WRITTEN BY
Barbara Shaw McKinney

PICTURES BY
Michael S. Maydak

I0802116

A DROP AROUND THE WORLD

THE SCIENCE OF THE WATER CYCLE

DAWN PUBLICATIONS
CONNECTING CHILDREN AND NATURE

sourcebooks eXplore

To my children, Robin and Reed, who have welcomed Raindrop into our family.
—BSMcK

To Beth, Wolf, and Teal.
—MSM

Text © 1998, 2021 by Barbara Shaw McKinney
Illustrations © 1998, 2021 by Michael Maydak
Cover design by Michelle Martinez
Cover and internal design © 2021 by Sourcebooks

Sourcebooks, Dawn Publications, and the colophon are registered trademarks of Sourcebooks.

All rights reserved.

The characters and events portrayed in this book are fictitious or are used fictitiously. Any similarity to real persons, living or dead, is purely coincidental and not intended by the author.

Published by Dawn Publications, an imprint of Sourcebooks eXplore
P.O. Box 4410, Naperville, Illinois 60567-4410
(630) 961-3900
sourcebookskids.com

Originally published in 1998 in the United States by Dawn Publications.

Library of Congress Cataloging-in-Publication Data is on file with the publisher.

Source of Production: Wing King Tong Paper Products Co. Ltd., Shenzhen, Guangdong Province, China
Date of Production: December 2021
Run Number: 5024618

Printed and bound in China.
WKT 30 29 28 27 26 25

Raindrop, take us to the skies.
Teach us how to vaporize.

Condense us so that we can flow
to places only raindrops go.

Cycle with us through the trees,
underground, beneath the seas.

Please explain the things you do,
your special tricks and changes too.

Perhaps some symbols could keep track
throughout this book, from front to back.

Now show us how you work and play.
Let's tour the world, the "raindrop way."

Then afterwards, when all is done,
we'll share your secrets, one by one.

P.S.
Drop, if we lose you, don't despair—
we'll find your face on each page somewhere.

Nestled in a cloud near Maine,
little Droplet longs to rain.
Though not yet big enough to fall,
it waits with others, still too small.

Then adventure starts to blow...
on wings of wind, it's off they go.
Sailing in an ocean cloud,
moisture feeds the droplet crowd.

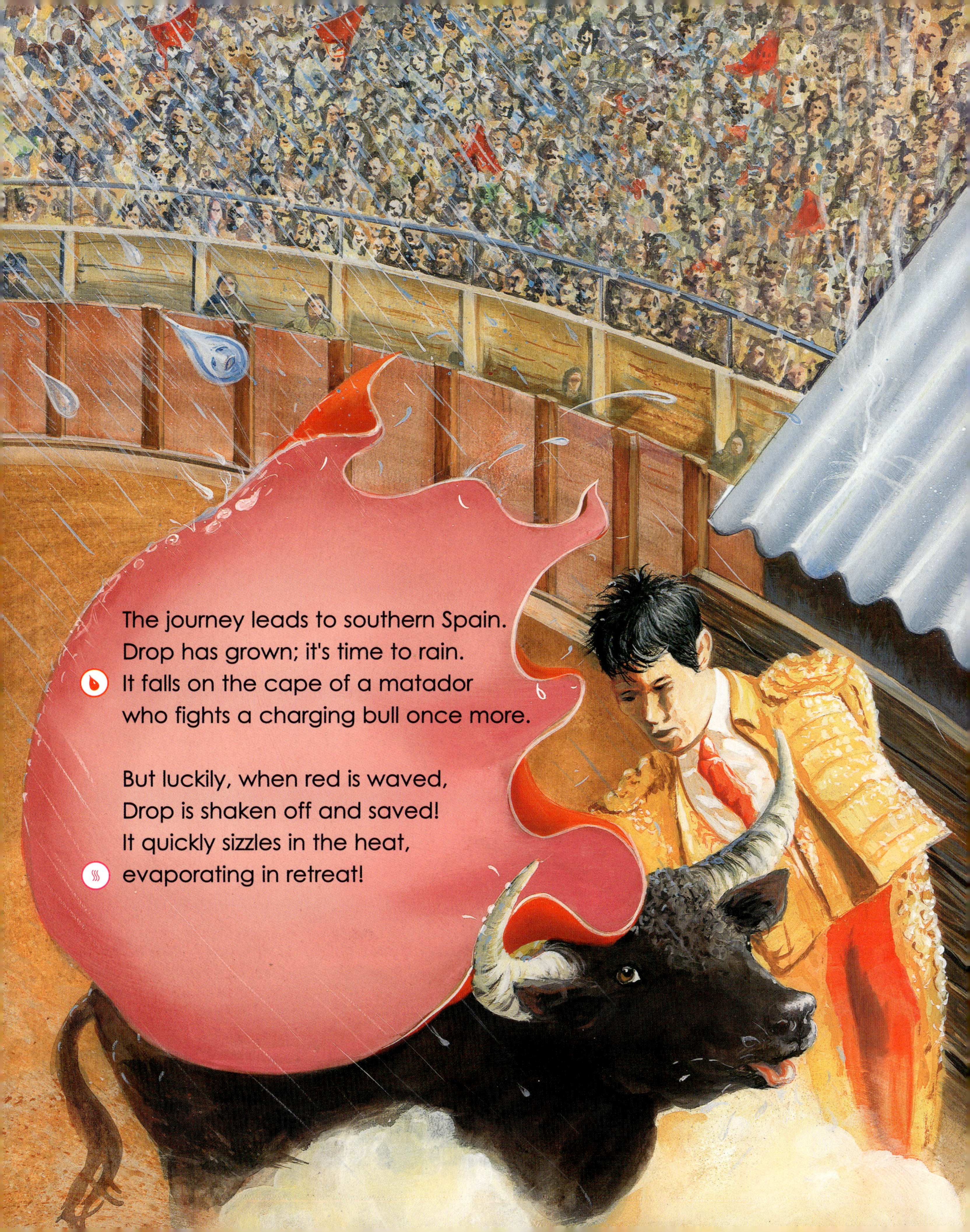

The journey leads to southern Spain.
Drop has grown; it's time to rain.
It falls on the cape of a matador
who fights a charging bull once more.

But luckily, when red is waved,
Drop is shaken off and saved!
It quickly sizzles in the heat,
evaporating in retreat!

Then off to Switzerland it flies,
mountain-climbing winter skies.
The vapor freezes in midair,
and magically a snowflake's there.

Alpine peaks all powdered white
invite the snow to spend the night.
This delicate and airy flake
drifts down on a frozen lake.

One April day it melts away,
meandering its way toward May.
Icy nights refreeze the drop.
Its solid state commands a stop.

But warmer mornings let it flow.
Stop-and-go, stop-and-go.
Finally our drop of rain
roars a river's glad refrain...

Free and fluid, flowing fast—
free and liquid, loose at last!

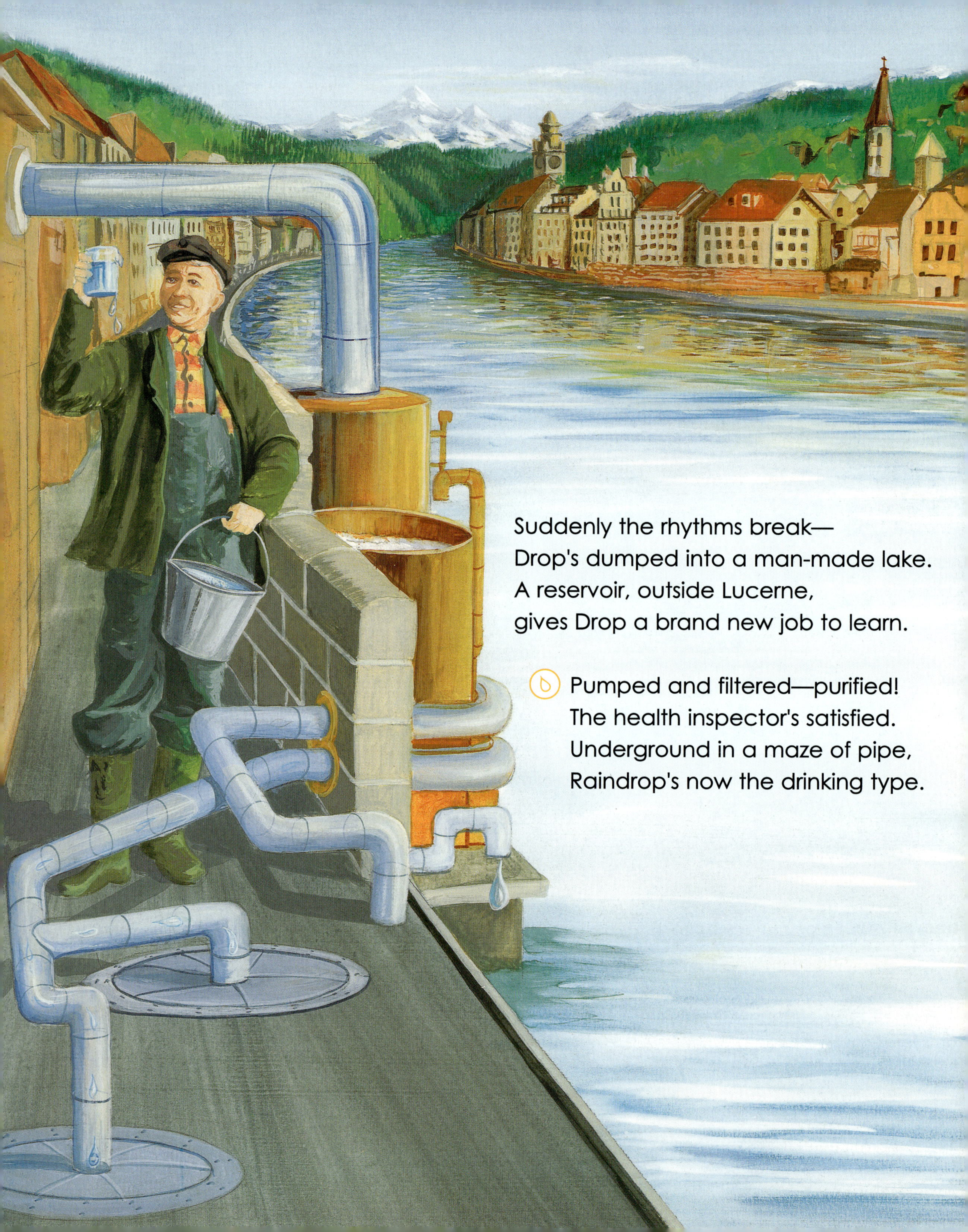

Suddenly the rhythms break—
Drop's dumped into a man-made lake.
A reservoir, outside Lucerne,
gives Drop a brand new job to learn.

Pumped and filtered—purified!
The health inspector's satisfied.
Underground in a maze of pipe,
Raindrop's now the drinking type.

It stops at a spigot, meets a dead end.
What's beyond, around the bend?
When the knob is turned, the secret's out!
Clean-water Drop pours out the spout.

Drop runs into a trough headfirst,
where cow laps up to quench her thirst.
Raindrop races through the cow
to glands that "milkify" somehow.

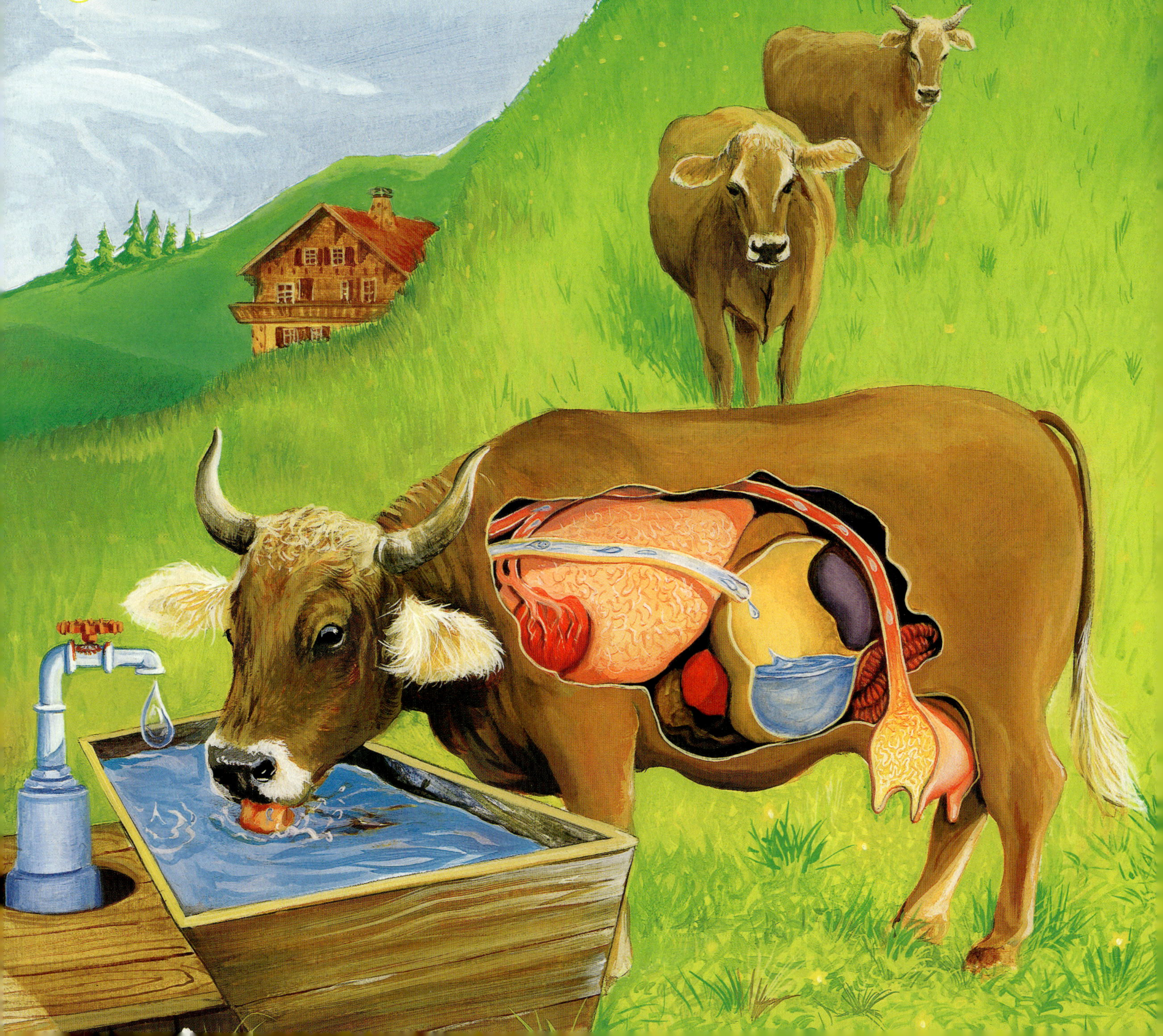

Mixed up in a pail of milk,
it's poured in a glass as smooth as silk,
but slips from Heidi's little hands
and forms a puddle where she stands.

Puddle Drop is warmed away
like a helium balloon at play.
Its milkiness is left behind—
vapor-pure, it's been refined.

Sunlight lifts it, oh so high,
to cirrus clouds that fly the sky.
Speeding south to desert lands,
Sahara waits with thirsty sands.

Sand dunes fold their hands in prayer,
pleading for some moister air.
But like a tease, our Drop blows by…
No, not a cloud stops by to cry.

As vapor adrift at a lazy pace,
Drop finds itself in a jungly place.
Water, water everywhere—
rainforests have such humid air.

The air is warm above the pools,
but over land it quickly cools.
This sudden change from warm to cool
turns Drop to fog; it's nature's rule.

Camouflaged in a ghostly sky,
it collides with a monkey swinging by.
Drop gets a lift on a curly tail
to a swimming hole on the jungle trail.

Gravity pulls at the drop.
Over the falls, it cannot stop!
Lost in a mist of colored spray,
that Drop is off without delay.

Overseas our Drop is sped
on electric flight in a thunderhead.
Monsoon winds forewarn Mumbai:
the Raindrop Army storms July!

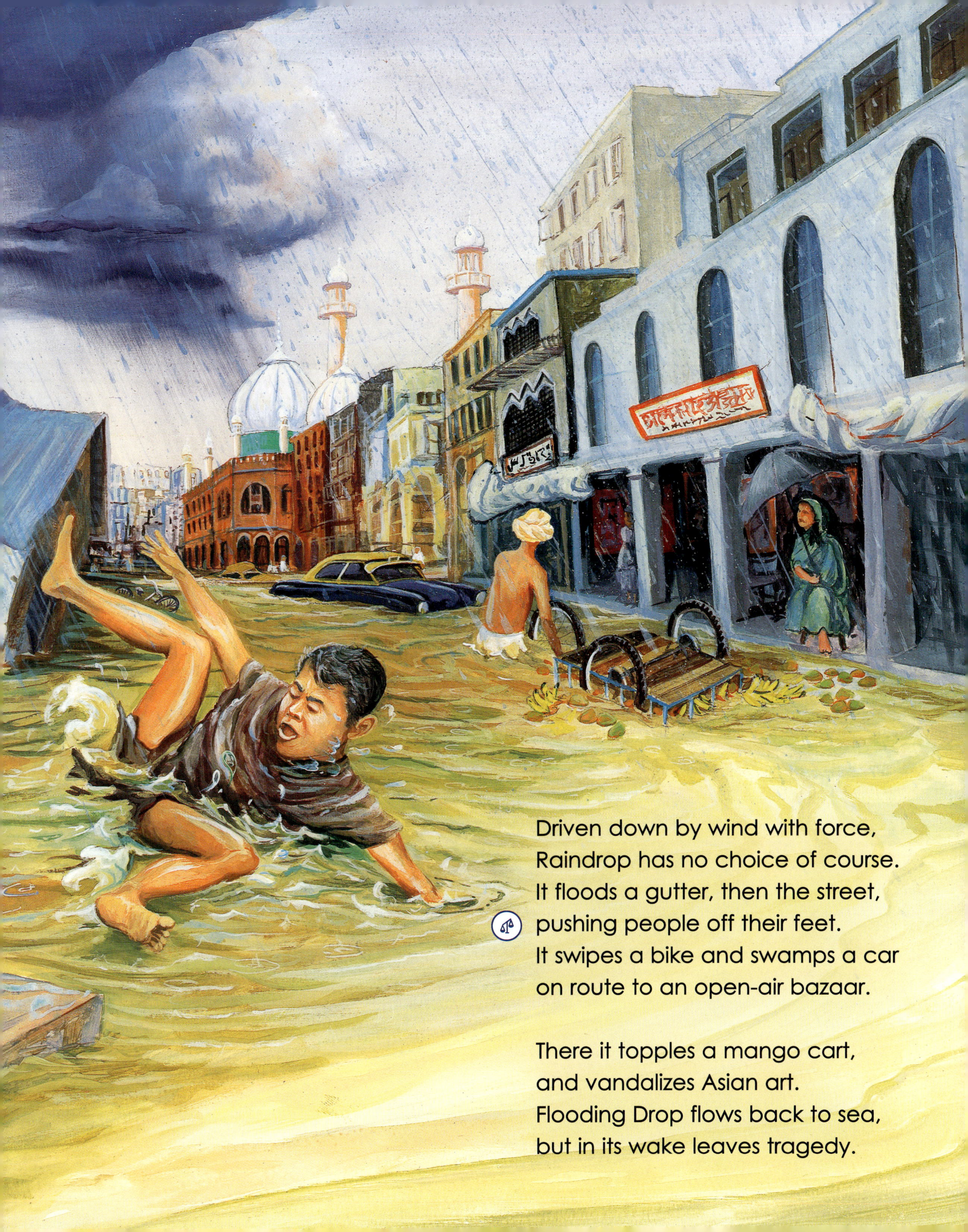

Driven down by wind with force,
Raindrop has no choice of course.
It floods a gutter, then the street,
pushing people off their feet.
It swipes a bike and swamps a car
on route to an open-air bazaar.

There it topples a mango cart,
and vandalizes Asian art.
Flooding Drop flows back to sea,
but in its wake leaves tragedy.

Drop takes a dive like a submarine—
an environmental life machine.
It's needed by the fish below
to fill their gills, to swim, to grow.

Hypnotized by the rolling motion,
it's lured down deeper in the ocean.
Weight is heavy on its shoulder,
squeezed in darkness, Drop is colder.

Drop surfs a wave to a coral reef—
reflecting color beyond belief!
There it gently laps the sand,
rocking back and forth to land.

Australian children come to play
by the water's edge this sunny day.
They build a tower, sail a boat.
Sea Drop fills their castle moat.

Shallow water warms up quick.
Drop does the disappearing trick!
Swinging on a breeze trapeze,
it's off to meet the Japanese.

In stratus style, without a doubt,
Drop'll burst its cloud and tumble out.
Drenching Drop makes gushy dirt,
a perfect mudpie for dessert.

On a mission, sinking deep,
through the cracks it tries to seep,
passing worms and bugs that creep
and animals curled up asleep.

Avoiding stones and bones that block,
it passes through some porous rock.
How far down? It's hard to tell.
Drop runs into a farmer's well.

There it waits till it's hoisted up
by bucket to a drinking cup.
That swallowed Drop is lost within,
yet finds an exit through the skin.

As a bead of sweat on a farmer's nose,
it drips off the tip to his working clothes.
Joined by a soap and water team,
Drop hangs on line and turns to steam.

Drop looks east to greet the west.
Pacific winds do all the rest.
Circling, cycling, drop is dizzy!
Changing weather keeps it busy!

Cumulus without a care…
Where will it go? It knows not where.
North winds quickly claim the cloud—
no dilly-dallying allowed!

Falling temperatures cause a change.
Freezing Drop starts feeling strange.
It flaunts a fancy, frosty face
and wears a coat of crystal lace.

It whirls and swirls in Arctic air
and hibernates with a polar bear.
Then much to our playful flake's delight,
two tiny cubs are born one night!
Together the snowflakes keep them warm,
a baby blanket in a storm.

Frozen land waits long for Spring.
At last it comes—a wondrous thing!
Melting snow and sunny days
dress tundra in a brilliant blaze.

Seeping in the thawing earth,
Drop finds a seed and gives it birth.
When buttercup is blooming bright,
Drop's exhaled in a vapor flight.

Next it rides the Jet Stream Express,
a thousand miles, more or less,
to downpour over Yellowstone,
which makes the tourists moan and groan.

But each drop's needed to make things grow
since the water table's running low.
Drop dissolves ingredients
like minerals and nutrients.

Sucked up the roots of an aspen tree,
it makes a fast food delivery.
It saves a life and brings relief,
then escapes through a hole beneath the leaf.

Evaporated once again!
Will it return? It knows not when.
Condensing on a speck of dust,
Drop heads home in a mighty gust.

New England weather brings surprises—
water's there in all disguises.
But cruising to the coast today,
Drop brings rain to Cape Cod Bay.

The sun peeks out through a patch of blue
before the passing shower's through.
Raindrops bend each ray of sun
like little prisms having fun.

They paint the sky with colors bright,
a miracle of hope and light.
Our Drop makes a wish from the rainbow aglow,
a hope for the future of mankind below...

"Let the children take care of the water on Earth,
conserve it, protect it, and value its worth."

A MAGIC SHOW STARRING H_2O

A SHOW ON THE ROAD

Raindrops are world travelers! As vapors, they ride air currents that sweep the skies from continent to continent. When falling from clouds as liquids or solids, they're brought to the ground by gravity. Water often travels far in underground streams. Eventually, rivers and streams bring it back to its source, the ocean, where currents carry it from sea to sea. The whole world is its playground.

TRANSFORMATION TRICKS

Water teams up with temperature to perform the most amazing tricks! Here's how they work together:

VANISHING VAPOR

Heat makes water molecules dance—the hotter the temperature, the faster they move. The faster they move, the more molecules bounce out of their drops as invisible water vapor. This flight of airborne water vapor is called evaporation. At a rock'n, roll'n 212 degrees Fahrenheit (F), which is the same as 100 degrees Celsius (C), the water molecules boil, bumping each other wildly into thin air.

CONDENSING COLD

Cooler temperature slows them down again and the molecules condense to a liquid—as rain, dew, or drops on the side of your cold glass. This is the mist you might see early in the morning either when cool air hits warmer air near the ground, or warm air hits cooler air close to the ground, depending on the season. The tiny droplets are quickly burned off when the sun warms them and they evaporate. The steamy rainforest cycles a lot of water, round and round beneath its canopy, so there's a lot of condensed water vapor in the air, appearing as mist.

FREEZING FAHRENHEIT

Falling temperatures slow them down even more, until at 32 degrees F, or 0 degrees C, the molecules huddle close together and almost stand still! When nearly motionless, their form changes from a fluid to a solid—ice or snow. Snow appears when water vapor freezes in midair. But if water vapor condenses into ice crystals when touching a very cold surface, like a windshield on a winter morning, we see frost. Warm them up to watch them flow again.

POLLUTION SOLUTION

Everybody loves sparkling clean water! But sometimes water gets polluted and dissolves things that shouldn't be there, so it must be purified. One way to solve this problem is to run water through a filter, trapping the unwanted things. Another way is to let the water evaporate, leaving the impurities behind. Then we can condense the pure water vapor by cooling it back into crystal clear water. This is called distilled water.

BODY BUDDY

Water sneaks in and out of your body every day, all the time, whether you know it or not. It soaks right into your skin when you get wet, and you even inhale it as vapor when you breathe! When you squeeze an orange and drink the juice, it mostly consists of water that the orange tree drank from the ground. And almost everything you eat has lots of water in it. An apple is about 84 percent water, a carrot is about 88 percent water, and lettuce is 95 percent water. Since milk is mostly water too, cows and other mammals must be sure to drink plenty of water, enough to nurse their young. But water is just a visitor—it is always leaving bodies too. Every time you exhale, perspire, cry, vomit, urinate, bleed, or blow your nose, some water says goodbye. Did you know that your body is 65 percent water? Everybody needs water—lots of it.

CLOUD MAKER

Drink plenty of water, then "huff" outside on a frosty morning. Warm vapor from your body hits cold air, condenses, and...presto! A tiny cloud! Similarly, the warm earth "breathes" warm air which rises, cools and...presto! A cloud is born.

- Low hanging gray clouds that blanket the sky are called stratus clouds. They bring rain.
- Puffy white cumulus clouds form higher up on fair weather days.
- Dark thunderheads called cumulonimbus clouds bring storms.
- Wispy cirrus clouds are made of ice crystals that form high up in the atmosphere where it's freezing cold. There, winds spread them like feathers across the sky.
- Fog is simply a cloud close to the ground.

HEAVY MAGIC

Water is heavy. If you've ever had to haul a bucket of water, you know how heavy it is—a pound for every pint. For this reason, deep sea divers must wear special equipment to withstand the great weight pressing down on them. The weight of water at three hundred feet down is ten times heavier than at the surface. In the deepest parts of the ocean, a piece of wood might actually compress to half its size under the tremendous pressure. Imagine how heavy the water in a waterfall must be! That's why the weight of rushing water is used to turn generators that make electricity. The next time you turn on a light, consider that water may be its secret source!

HOME SWEET HOME

To life beneath the sea, water is everything. Water is up, down, and everywhere. Water gives oxygen. Water gives food. Water gives everything needed for life. Water is more than just a substance—it's a place called home.

TEMPERATURE TAMER

What's the biggest difference between Earth and Mars, Jupiter, or any other planet? Answer: Earth is the water planet! Unlike other planets, Earth has lots of water in all three forms: solid, liquid, and gas. Most important, Earth's perfect distance from the sun lets water flow as a liquid. Water on planets closer to the sun would evaporate in the great heat. Water on planets farther away from the sun would freeze in the extreme cold. In all three states, but especially as a liquid, water helps to keep Earth's temperature moderate. Unlike land, which heats up quickly in the sun but cools off just as fast at night, water absorbs the sun's heat slowly and stores it for a long time before returning it to the air. During the daytime, the oceans, rivers, and lakes absorb the sun's heat slowly, so it's not too hot. At night, they give heat back to the air, little by little, so it's usually not too cold for living things. As a gas, water further protects us with clouds of water vapor that both shield the Earth from the daytime sun and hold heat in like a nighttime blanket. As a solid, a blanket of snow keeps hibernating animals warm in winter by preventing the escape of body heat into the cold air above ground. It's also a shelter from wind chill, keeping snow caves and even igloos cozy inside.

SUPER SOAKER

Where does all the rainfall go? Some of it evaporates, some flows downhill in streams and rivers to the ocean, and a lot of it is soaked up by a giant sponge called the Earth. Silently it journeys underground until it gurgles out through a natural hole called a spring. Or it might be pumped out of a man-made hole called a well.

THE GREEN MACHINE

Water keeps our Earth green and healthy! Seeds need water to sprout and become plants. Water usually flows down, but plants draw it up through roots, stems, and tree trunks! Like a magic potion, it dissolves vitamins from the soil, transports them up into the plant, and works with sunshine to make food in the leaves. When its job is done, it's breathed out through little holes under the leaves as vapor in a process called transpiration. When plants need new water, they beg for a drink by drooping.

DISSOLVIN' SOLVENT

In the blink of an eye, clean water changes its colorless, tasteless, odorless self into the color, taste, and fragrance of things it dissolves. Water jiggles in gelatin, bubbles in the bath, and tastes fruity in tropical punch. It dissolves Easter egg dye, powdered milk, and even the minerals in rock. And of course, water dissolves soap, and together this dynamic duo dissolves dirt! Yes, water is the world's best solvent.

STUPENDOUS BEND-ABILITY

Water can do a remarkable thing—it can bend light. This refraction fools us about the size and location of underwater objects. When water vapor in the sky bends sunlight after a rain, light is split into all of its colors—called the spectrum—and we are treated to a rainbow.

BARBARA SHAW MCKINNEY is a teacher as well as a poet. She was inspired to use the magic of children's literature to spark her students' curiosity about the wonders of water. She vowed to "turn a drop of rain into a drop of life, astounding children by its eternity." Her sprightly verse elicits a "water-wow!" in this, her first book. From Manchester, Connecticut, McKinney draws on her experience as a mother, musician, and curriculum developer to promote quality education through workshops for teachers.

MICHAEL S. MAYDAK regularly gets waist or chest deep in water, pursuing one of his passions: fly fishing in the lakes and streams of the wild West. When he isn't out in it, he's likely to be painting nature in the studio of his home in Cool, California, where he lives with his wife and two children. Maydak has been a professional artist since 1976. He previously illustrated the book *Lifetimes* for Dawn Publications.